Table of Contents

Introduction

Artificial Intelligence is a field that has a long history but has continued to grow and change. It is a powerful driving force in changing humanity by assisting businesses and people generate exciting, creative products and services, make critical decisions, and attain major goals. This is the reason why organizations keep hiring AI experts at a jaw-dropping speed.

The median salary of an AI developer in the US is not less than $80,000 based on payscale.com. Virtually all great tech companies run an artificial intelligence project and are ready to cash out millions of dollars to assist in completing the project.

Approximately 13.6 million jobs will emerge in the AI field in the next decade. However, there is a staggering shortage of talent in AI. For example, there are less than 10,000 people in the world with the skill set sufficient to carry out a significant research.

Artificial Intelligence (AI) technology is highly popular in our daily lives. It has applications in different sectors right from gaming, media to finance, and also the state-of-the-art research industries from medical diagnosis, robotics, and quantum science. The Artificial Intelligence Book for beginners focuses on driving an interest in its learners in the field of AI so that they are ready to learn more advanced topics in the same field.

The introduction to AI explains the background history of artificial intelligence, robotics, learning methods of Artificial Intelligence, basics of modern AI, and some representative of applications of AI. Along the way, we also plan to excite you about the huge possibilities in the field of AI, which continues to drive human ability beyond our imagination.

Chapter 1: Background to Artificial Intelligence

Can Machines Think Like We Humans?

The first part of the 20th century was the time when science fiction started to introduce the concept of artificially intelligent robots. This began with the "Tin Man" from the Wizard of Oz and went on with the impersonated Maria Metropolis.

When the 1950s arrived, there was already a crop of scientists, philosophers, and mathematicians with the idea of artificial intelligence penetrated into their minds.

One example of this person is a young British polymath called Alan Turing who said that human beings make use of existing information to reason and solve problems. And so, machines can also do the same. This illustrated his logic in a paper dated 1950 called "Computing Machinery and Intelligence" which explained how one can create intelligent machines and measure their intelligence too.

Make Pursuit Possible

Unfortunately, it is very easy and cheap to speak. Turing couldn't implement this concept during that time. Well, some of the reasons which stopped Turing from putting his idea into action include a need for computers to change. If you were to trace back and look at the 1949 computers, there were many improvements and discoveries which are required to be done. These computers lacked the fundamental element of intelligence. It was very hard to instruct this computer to execute any command. In short, the 1950s computers couldn't send commands to implement or remember whatever they did. Secondly, computing was not cheap but very expensive. For example, the cost of hiring a computer was around $200, 000 per month. Only the biggest universities and large tech companies could afford to spend such a huge amount of money. The need to prove a concept and effort from highly influential people is what was needed to convince funding sources that

Artificial Intelligence was a great field worth to pursue.

The Conference that Sounded the Bell

After five years, evidence to support the concept of Artificial Intelligence was realized through Allen Newell, Herbert Simon, and Cliff Shaw's Logic Theorist. This was a program which had been designed with the aim to emulate how to solve problems of a human being and get funding from the Research and Development Corporation. Many see it as the first program of artificial intelligence that was presented at the Dartmouth Summer Research Project on Artificial Intelligence that was hosted by John McCarthy and Marvin Minsky.

In this conference, McCarthy united top researchers from different fields and allowed them to have an open-ended discussion on Artificial Intelligence which was used at the same event. Unfortunately, this conference didn't live up to McCarthy's expectations. People came and walked away as they pleased and they did not agree on standard methods for the field. However, everyone who attended was in agreement with the statement that AI is achievable. This was only the most positive thing from this conference. But the importance of this event could not be ignored because it triggered research into AI.

The Road to Success and Setbacks

Between 1957 and 1974, AI rapidly developed. Computers were designed that had the ability to store a lot of information and process information faster. New machine learning algorithms were developed and people got enlightened to know which type of algorithm to choose to solve their problem.

Examples by Newell and Simon's General Problem Solver were great examples to show the goals of problem-solving and interpretation of spoken language. Such success and the advocacy by top researchers made the government agencies to begin to fund in Artificial Intelligence research. The government was very interested in a machine that could transcribe and translate spoken language.

In 1970, Marvin Minsky talked to Life Magazine and predicted that three to eight years from then, there will be a machine that has the general intelligence of an average human being. While there was a basic proof of concept, the journey was still long before this could be achieved.

To achieve AI, there were several obstacles experienced. The biggest problem was the lack of a computational power to execute anything significant. For example, computers didn't store enough information and process it fast. For communication to take place, it was important to understand the definition and meaning of words. Hans Moravec was McCarthy's doctoral student during that time, he stated the following "computers were still millions of times too weak to exhibit intelligence." People started to lose patience and this then affected the funding, and soon research slowed down for about ten years.

Later in the 1980s, AI was brought to the limelight by two sources. One included the extension of the algorithmic toolkit and a raise of funds. Both Rumelhart and John Hopfield were the key people who started to spread the idea of "deep learning" techniques that created room for computers to learn by experience.

Conversely, Edward Feigenbaum created an expert system with the ability to mimic the decision-making process of a human expert.

The program could ask an expert how to respond to a particular situation, and once this was learned for virtually every incidence, people who are not experts could gain advice from a program. Expert systems were largely used in industries.

The Japanese government accorded a lot of support to expert systems and other advances in AI developments. Between 1982-1990, the Japanese invested $400 million dollars with the focus to revolutionize computer processing, implement a logic program, and enhance artificial intelligence. However, the set goals were not achieved. But one can argue that the indirect effects of Fifth Generation Computer Project inspired the talented young generation of engineers and scientists.

Even with the lack of government funding, AI did not die. In fact, between

1990 and 2000, many goals of artificial intelligence were achieved. In 1997, the world chess champion was defeated by a computerized chess program. This highly popularized match was the first time that a world chess champion had been defeated by a computer chess program. This was a big step towards the creation of an artificially intelligent decision-making program.

In the same period, other developments were also witnessed such as a speech recognition program created by Dragon Systems. This program was installed and run on windows. This was another big step realized in the field of spoken language interpretation. Soon, it seemed like there was no problem which machines couldn't solve. For example, emotions of human beings were illustrated by the Kismet robot. This robot had the ability to detect and show human emotions.

Time is the Healer of All Wounds

Still, how artificial intelligence could be programmed was a nightmare. So what might have changed? Well, it turns out that the biggest computer storage limitation which seemed to prevent researchers 30 years ago was not at all a problem. For example, it was approximated that the memory and speed of computers doubled each year. This is actually how Deep Blue eclipsed Garry Kasparov in 1997. It is the same way in which Google's Alpha Go defeated Chinese Go champion, Kie Je. This seems to explain the roller coaster of AI research.

Artificial Intelligence is Everywhere

As of today, we are in the era of "big data, "a time when humans have the ability to gather big sums of information that is impossible for a human being to process. The application of artificial intelligence has been a significant success in many industries like entertainment, marketing, and banking. Although algorithms can't do a lot, both big and massive computing will facilitate artificial intelligence to learn using brute force.

Top Example Application of Artificial Intelligence

Artificial Intelligence and Quantum

Computing

The fact is that no one can stop AI from evolving. Humans have continued to focus on enhancing life across each spectrum, and the application of technology has turned out to be an engine for achieving that. While the past 100 years might be seen as the most dramatic technological upheavals to life compared to all human history, the coming 100 years are going to create a way for the multi-generational.

This shall be at the hands of Artificial Intelligence which has become smarter, more-fluid, and faster because of Quantum computing. The Quantum computers have been designed to solve life's most complex challenges and mysteries related to aging, poverty, war, famine, and many other things.

Beyond the application of Quantum-computing, the current A.I systems have advanced machine learning programs with massive behavioral algorithms which suit themselves to the likes and dislikes. Although it is largely useful, these machines aren't going to get smarter in an existential way, but they shall enhance their skills and usefulness depending on the dataset. There are a few popular examples of artificial intelligence being applied today. For example:

1. Siri

If you are a lover of Apple, then you must be familiar with Siri — a personal assistant. She has a friendly voice that she uses to interact with users daily. She helps Apple users discover information, give directions, add events to their calendars, send messages, and many other things. In short, Siri is a pseudo-intelligent digital personal assistant. She applies machine learning technology to respond to users.

2. Alexa

Alexa shocked many when it emerged to become the smart home's hub. Introduced and created by Amazon. One of its strongest unique ability is to decipher speech from any place in the room, set alarms, schedule appointments, and also power smart homes.

3. Tesla

If you don't have a Tesla, then you have no clue what you are missing. This is one of the best cars that have ever been designed. Not because many people have expressed the beauty of the vehicle but its predictive ability, self-driving features and the technological "coolness" it brings. If you are into cars, then you need to go get an experience of Tesla cars.

4. Cogito

This is one of the best examples of behavioral adaptation to help enhance the emotional intelligence of customer support representatives found on the market today. The company is an integration of machine learning and behavioral science to boost customer interaction for phone professionals.

5. Boxever

This is a company which deals a lot with machine learning to help enhance the experience of the customer in the travel industry and supply micro-moments that satisfies customers along the way. It is via machine learning and application of A.I that the company has domineered the playing field. This helps customers to discover new methods of engaging their customers in the playing field.

6. Netflix

Netflix has an advanced predictive technology depending on customer's reactions to films. It will analyze billions of records to recommend films which you might like depending on the previous choices and reactions to films. This tech is increasingly getting smarter every year as the size of the dataset increases.

Chapter 2: Robotics

Nearly everywhere you go now you'll see Artificial Intelligence implemented. On the screens, pockets, and who knows maybe one day it might be walking to a home near you. The headlines tend to strike this extensive field into a single subject. Robots being developed from labs, algorithms playing traditional games and winning, AI and some of the things which it can achieve are becoming part of our everyday lives. Although most of these incidences have a specific link to AI, this is not at all a monolithic field, but one that has many different disciplines.

Artificial intelligence and photonics have made it possible to develop robots using new methods of linking business, medicine, and many other applications. There is no argument that the age of robot has come upon us. The idea of robots might bring to mind important androids such as C-3PO in "Star Wars" and Rosie from "The Jetsons". It might even send fears to human beings because advanced robots continue to become better and indispensable. Most of these robots have now assumed dangerous or boring jobs done by human beings. Whichever the case, many people haven't come to realize the ubiquitous nature of robots because, in many incidences, the robots are less Android and resemble industrial tools. Integrating photonics technology such as sensors, lasers, and facial recognition technology, robotics exist in every field starting from industrial processing devices like Google's self-driving car.

Based on the International Federation of Robotics (IFR), the year 2013 witnessed an increased sale of industrial robots in the chemical, automotive, and food processing industries. The automotive sector contains one-third of all industrial robots that help in car manufacturing. IFR estimates that between 2012 and 2013, the global call for personal and domestic service robots increased to $1.7 billion.

The classic nature of robots has resulted in a huge progress too. For instance, when it was announced that a hotel in Japan would be provided with a human-like robot, the concept of fleshy humanoid robots from the "Future

World" or "Westworld" started to become a reality.

The "Henn-na Hotel in Nagasaki Prefecture", translated to "Strange Hotel" was to be supplied with receptionist robots that have a strong human likeness. These robots had to greet visitors and involve them in intelligent conversations. Robots were also to provide room service, housekeeping, and porter service.

Another robot that is less human and more logical is the Baxter series of robots at Rethink Robotics Inc. in Boston. Baxter has a good interactive platform that combines 360 sonar sensors and personalized software. Baxter operates even though there are great workers who can optimize the research and manufacturing process. Baxter's camera support application of computer vision using a 30-fps image capture rate and great resolution of 640 x 400 pixels.
During the launch of the Australian Centre for Robotic Vision, Sue Keay, the chief operating officer at ACRV said that the robotic vision is main technology which will support robotics to transform labor-intensive industries and obstruct with stagnating markets. This will then turn robots into a ubiquitous feature of the current world.

That being said, let's learn some deep concepts about robotics. So, what do you think is a robot? Well, you can pick any definition which you think is right for you, but we shall define a robot as "a device which performs work." And I guess you know what work is. If not, work is the exertion of energy. As you can see, the definition of a robot is open to anything that is non-human.

We aren't going to judge whether the robot is going to perform an important task. How important the robot is can be determined by the creator. And your robot doesn't need to have two legs which it can walk for it to be considered a robot.

Now you can see that at one point in your life, you have used robots but didn't realize that. For example, a vending machine is a great example of a robot. Other examples include a washing machine and dishwasher. Don't forget the automatic checkout lane found in a grocery. In other words, robots are always around us and you aren't supposed to fear them.

The function of a robot is to perform a given a task. So it should always have a means in which it can execute tasks. The technique to complete a task arises from its controlling mechanism and structure.

The Structure

The structure refers to the physical components. A robot can have one or more physical parts that assume a specific motion to perform a task. Take the example of a vending machine. It contains motorized spiral things which push the product out. The dishwasher contains a water-spraying arm that sprays water on the dishes. A washing machine contains motor which rotates the drum that holds clothes.

Control

For an action to take place, the structure must have control. Your robot will remain in one position unless you provide a control technique. The vending machine has a control panel that will let a customer pay for a given product. Dishwasher and washing machine have control panels and buttons. If you look at the automatic checkout lane, it contains a touchscreen control with an interface.

Types of Control

Robots have two types of control. There is the external control and internal control. For robots that are controlled externally, there is a different entity which seems to control it. On the other hand, internally controlled robots are autonomous. This means that it controls itself. As such, its controller is located inside the structure. The controller decides what steps or actions to do next on its own without any interference. For the external control, there are power switches and various configuration buttons. But once the internally-controlled robot is on, it performs the work on its own without any human interference.

Humanoid robots such as Honda's Asimo are autonomous. For the autonomous robots, there should be a means to detect their environment before decisions are made. This means that they have one sensor. Still, every autonomous robot can have different types of microcontroller installed inside. Many but not all externally controlled robots have a microcontroller inside. There are various types of microcontrollers that have different names. Usually, it keeps changing. At the center of a microcontroller, you will find a microprocessor core.

Popular cores are found in many products and have many followers. By learning how to program popular cores, it can give you a great opportunity to land a job in programming with a reputed company. For that reason, developers and programmers for popular cores are in high demand.

The core microprocessor is the main structure in the internal controller. The controller may not run a function if it doesn't have a software. Your robot's software could be predetermining. This means that you might not require to program it. But you may need to configure it by setting up some input switches before you control your robot with an external controller.

Now that you have learned some basic about robots, you can begin to think about how you can use this knowledge to even learn more.

Artificial Intelligence and Robots

In the first two decades of the 21st century, there has been an expansion of 'autonomous technology' and 'artificial intelligence'. Drones, self-driving cars, space exploration, software agents, and deep learning in medical diagnosis are among the most popular examples of areas where artificial intelligence has redefined. Artificial Intelligence in the form of machine learning and the presence of extensive datasets are some of the life domains which have driven development.

The unification of these digital technologies has even made them more powerful. AI installed in these systems can help redefine or improve conditions for humans and reduce the need for human contribution and interference during operation. Therefore, it is replacing humans with smart technology in hard, dirty, boring, and dangerous work.

Without any direct human intervention and external control, smart systems can facilitate dialogue with customers in online call-centers, drive robot hands to choose and manipulate objects accurately, purchase and sell stock at large quantities in a twinkle of an eye.

Despite this, it is sad that some of the most powerful cognitive tools are mostly opaque. Their actions aren't programmed by humans in a linear sequence. Google Brain designs AI which presumably builds AI better than human beings.

Chapter 3: Reinforcement Learning

Reinforcement learning is one of those topics that is widely discussed, contemplated, and researched in Artificial Intelligence because it has the ability to change most businesses. This section will look at reinforcement learning and further provide some practical examples of areas where it is used today.

What is Reinforcement Learning?

At the heart of reinforcement learning is the idea that the maximum behavior or action is enhanced by a positive reward.

Just like toddlers who begin to learn to walk have to adjust actions depending on the results they experience like taking a smaller step if the earlier step made them fall or knock something, machines and software agents have reinforcement learning algorithms which help choose the correct behavior depending on the previous feedback from the environment. As you can see, this is another form of machine learning and at the same time a branch of artificial intelligence.

Going by the complexity and nature of the problem, algorithms created for reinforcement learning can continue to adapt to the environment over time to take advantage of the reward in the long-term. Similar to the teetering toddler, a robot that is attempting to learn how to walk using reinforcement learning will attempt different ways to fulfill the objective, and receive feedback about how successful those methods are and then adjust until that point when the purpose to walk is realized. Making a big step forward causes the robot to fall, so it can adjust its step to ensure that it is smaller to test whether that is the way of maintaining stability.

It can proceed with learning through making different small steps until it is able to walk. In this case, the end reward is to stay upright, while the punishment is to fall. Depending on the feedback, the robot actions are reinforced.

Reinforcement learning requires a lot of data, and that is the reason why first applications in this technology have fields where simulated data is easily available.

Definitions of Reinforcement Learning

You can understand reinforcement learning by applying the idea of actions, agents, environments, and rewards. You will learn more about these terms shortly.

Capital letters represent a set of items and the lower-case letters denote an instance of a particular thing. For example, A describes all possible actions which represent a particular action in a set.

- **Agent**: An **agent** will select an action.

- **Action (A):** A is the set of all possible moves the agent can create.

- **Discount Factor:** This is multiplied by the agent to dampen the following rewards on choice of the agent's action.

- **Environment:** It describes the surrounding environment of the agent. Environment will accept the present state of the agent and action as input. The output is the reward of the agent and the next state.

- **State (S):** This describes the immediate situation that the agent discovers itself. This could be a specific moment and place.

- **Reward (R):** It is the feedback you can use to gauge the failure or success of an agent's actions.

- **Policy:** It is an approach which an agent uses to define the next action depending on the present state. It combines states to actions, the actions that have the best rewards.

- **Value (V):** It is the long-term return outcome that is expected instead of the short-term reward R.

- **Q-Value:** Resembles value but it has an additional parameter.

- **Trajectory:** Describes a sequence of actions and states that affect those states.

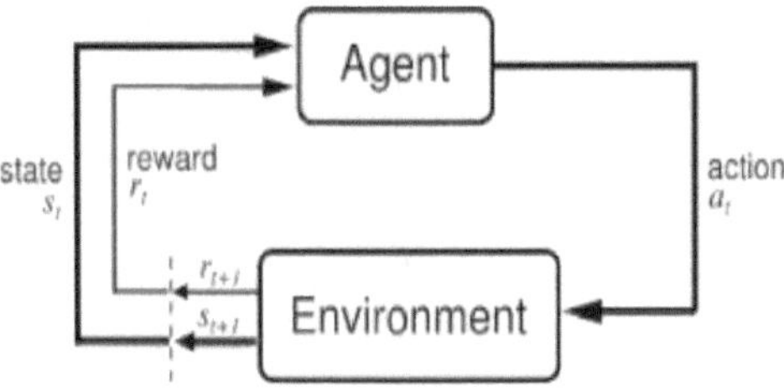

The feedback loop indicated above subscript refers to time steps t and t + 1. Each subscript explains various states. We have the current state t and t + 1. While other categories of machine learning such as supervised and unsupervised learning can be trained based on the state-action pairs, reinforcement learning determines actions based on the results it displays. In other words, it is a goal-oriented type of learning that learns a series of actions that make an agent achieve a particular goal.

Additionally, the difference between reinforcement learning and other types of learning-supervised and unsupervised learning is based on the way it interprets inputs.

- Unsupervised learning: The algorithm will learn similarities and through extension, it can sport the inverse and carry out any anomaly detection by identifying any unusual thing.

- Supervised learning: This is where the algorithm will learn corrections between instances of data and their labels.

- Reinforcement learning: This is where actions depend on short and long-term rewards.

Domain Selection for Reinforcement Learning

One approach which you can use to understand more about autonomous reinforcement learning agent is to imagine a person who is blind trying to walk around the world with ears and a white cane. The agents have a small room which gives them a chance to respond to their surroundings. However, this room may not be the best technique for them to identify whatever that is around them.

Additionally, to make a choice between the type of feedback and input which your agent has to deal with is a great challenge. Algorithms that are trained to play video games can skip this problem because of the environment.

As a result, video games create a sterile environment of the lab. This is the right time to test concepts on reinforcement learning. The human mind is a prerequisite domain selection, especially on matters about theories and knowledge of a given problem that should be solved.

The State-Action Pairs and Complex Probability Distribution

The goal of reinforcement learning is to select the best action for any particular state. In this case, actions are ranked and allocated values. Since the majority of the actions depend on a given state, you therefore need to measure the value of the state-action pairs.

This means that actions should be ranked and assigned values relative to each other. Since most of these actions depend on the state, what you are supposed to measure is the value of state-action pairs.

With reinforcement learning, you get the chance to model a complex probability distribution reward with respect to a massive state-action pair. For that reason, this particular type of learning goes hand in hand with a Markov decision process.

Reinforcement learning is iterative. It is commonly used to discover reward state-action pairs.

Machine Learning and Time

An algorithm is a method that you can take to aggregate lessons of time. The reinforcement learning algorithms have a special link to time. An algorithm can use the same state to test different actions until that time when it can attain the best action. Additionally, algorithms have a Groundhog Day where it acts dumb but continue to become wise with time.

Given that human beings have never experienced a Groundhog Day, reinforcement learning algorithms can learn a lot and work better than human beings. Therefore, the advantageous point of these algorithms over human beings is their ability to work parallel.

Deep Reinforcement Learning and Neural Networks

Neural networks are agents which learn to map a specific state-action and pair rewards. Not different to other neural networks, it contains coefficients which estimate the function which associates inputs and outputs.

When it comes to reinforcement learning, you can use convolutional networks to identify an agent's state. This means that it implements the task of image recognition. But convolutional networks run different interpretations from images in the reinforcement learning to supervised learning.

Chapter 4: Computer Vision

To teach a computer to learn how to see is not an easy task. Yes! You can connect a camera on a PC but that won't make it see. For a device to see the world the way people or animals do, it has to rely on computer vision and image recognition.

Therefore, computer vision is the reason why the barcode scanner can identify a set of stripes in a UPC. Additionally, this is how Apple's Face ID can determine whether a face that a camera has captured is yours.

Generally, when a device processes raw visual input like JPEG file, it can use computer vision to understand whatever it is seeing. It is easy for a person to look at computer vision as the part of the human brain that processes information that the eyes receive, rather than the eyes themselves.

An important function of computer vision from the AI perspective is the image recognition which provides the machine with the ability to describe the input received through computer vision and categorize everything that it sees.

Below are examples of image recognition work.

- The eBay application that has a camera to use to search items.

- Facebook's AI knows much about your photos.

- Neural networks changes pitch black photos into bright images.

- An AI program that can read the human mind.

There are also mobile applications which use a camera to determine whether an object is a hotdog or not. An example of this app is the NotHotdog. This app applies computer vision and image recognition to generate judgments. While it may not be a very attractive app, the process of training a neural network to run image recognition is complex both in the human brain and computers.

A computer vision has a sense of sight that is different from that understanding of the physical universe. And that is the reason why training is very important. It is similar to how a child is trained to identify numbers and letters. Children must be shown a number or letter several times so that they can recognize the number.

Still, many kids can quickly recognize numbers and letters while upside down once they can identify it in the upright position. Humans have a strong biological neural network that describes visual information.

The way image recognition works depends on the development of a neural network that processes individual image pixels. Researchers train these networks to allow them to identify similar images.

For instance, in the case of the hotdog, developers can feed an AI program with thousands of hotdog pictures. This particular AI can then develop a general idea of how a picture of a hotdog appears. If you supply it with an image, it has to compare with each pixel of that image with a hotdog image. If the input matches with the pixels of the image, AI defines it as a hot dog.

How AI Recognize An Image

Convolutional Neural Network drives computer vision technology. All data in a computer is read as a series of o and 1. Additionally, it has a wide variety of computational method to display different results. First, let's see how a computer reads an image using the ConvNet.

At one point in our lives, we have been "artists". During this time, we built and drew colored figures by using various shades that have a beautiful texture. The way you can differentiate things with your eyes is by how you perceive color. Consider an example of different colors on the pallet. There are different colors that have been tested and mixed to create a darker, light shade of color depending on the ratio used.

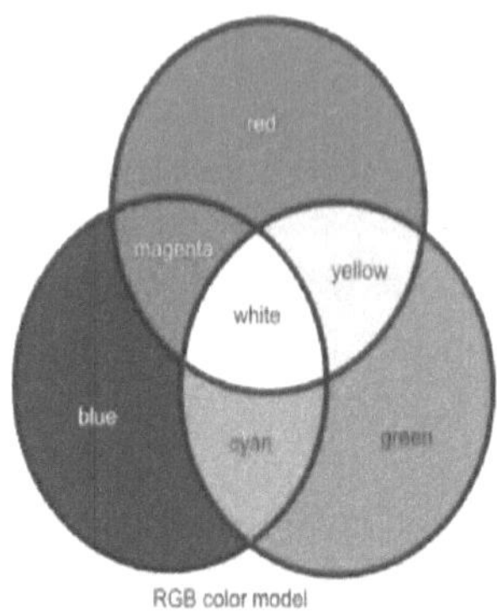

In the same way, Artificial Intelligence reads the above colors with a range of values from 0 to 255. The image above shows how you can apply the combination to remember the six major colors. It is referred to as the RGB model. In this case, Red, Green, and Blue are the dominant colors. Once they are combined together, another set of colors is developed (Cyan, Yellow, and Magenta).

The image below represents an experience. This describes a visual perception which defines white as a mix of different colors.

What is Seen by a Computer

Computer images have three important colors — red, blue, and green. There are several models applied in the computer vision field. In this section, you'll be introduced to a simple RGB model which describes how a computer can detect an image.

The RGB model is one of the oldest color differentiation tool found in the computer vision field. Since each major color has a value between 0 -255, a color with a high value implies that it is a brighter color. Next, let's divide each color into a subcategory which generates a color pallet.

Traverse from 0 to 255

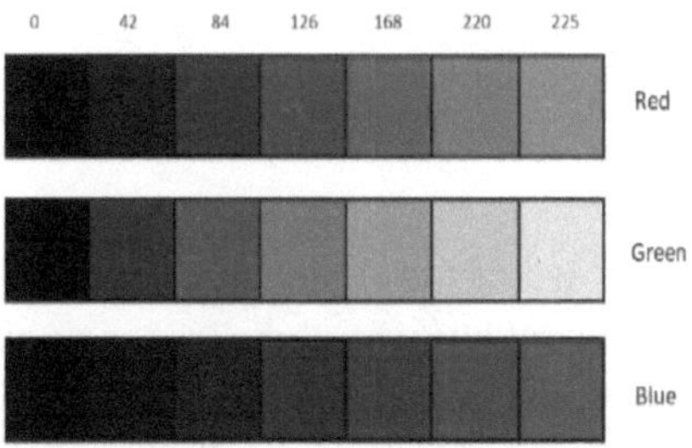

In the above image, each blue, red, and green color represents a particular shade of color. AI uses these numbers to interpret and process the image. When you combine two colors, for example, red and green, the final result is yellow. The yellow color is represented in three-dimensional space such as 255, 255, 0 (R.G.B). And so, RGB makes it possible to look at various colors like Cyan, Yellow, and Magenta.

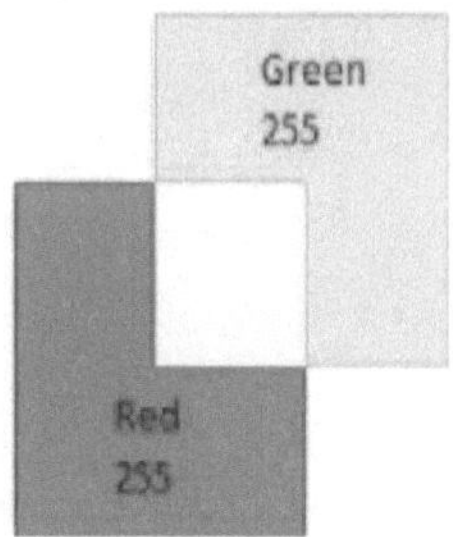

Images are made up of pixels which are close to another. The colored pixels have three channels organized one behind the other. All the channels operate together to display a specific color. Let's see how AI reads an image. If you implement the RGB model, you'll be able to extract more than 16 million shades of colors.

Values of a Pixel in an Image

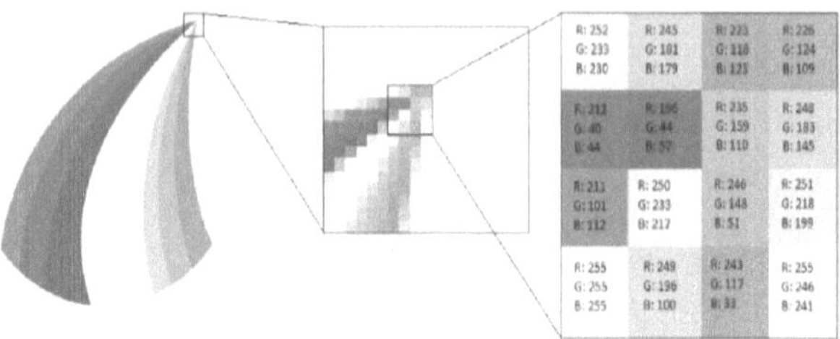

The above image is composed of three channels which are arranged one behind the other. Let's find out how the above channels are arranged to help find a pixelated image such the one shown above.

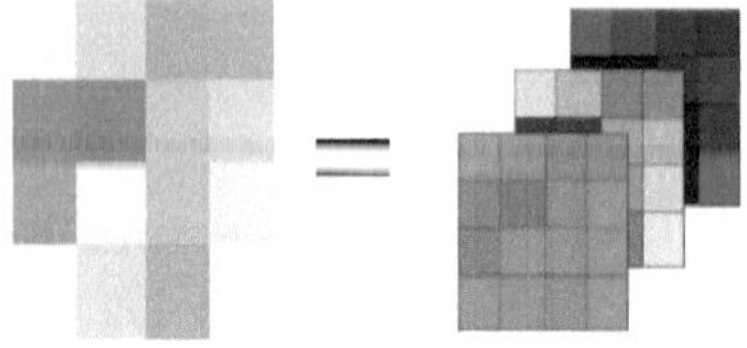

Image Recognition using ConvNet

Given that AI knows the pixel of each image, it can extract the values of RGB and keep it in memory. It begins by searching for a match of images that are similar and found in the database. Well, how is this whole process done?

In ML, ConvNet represents a complex feed-forward neural network. Why it is applied in classification and image recognition is because of the better accuracy.

The ConvNet sticks to a model which operates on creating a network and can send out a complete layer that has all interconnected neurons.

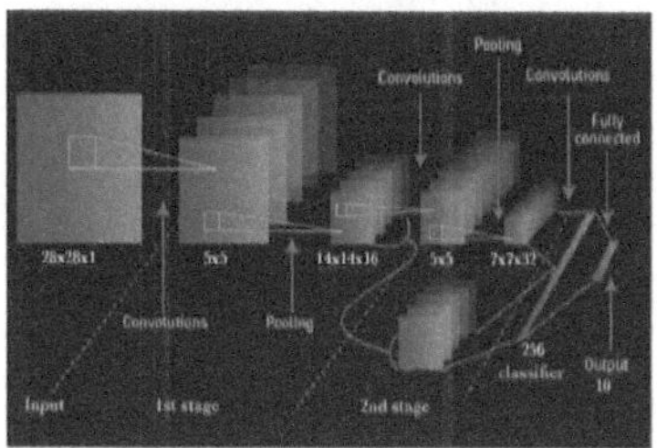

During the process of training of ConvNet, the hidden layer is the point at which the image is broken down. This is referred to as convolution. Each image comprises of an nxm number of pixels with a specific depth. In the ConvNet, the images are divided into two processes. Those two processes include filtering and pooling.

Filtering is the process that results in the transfer of a weight matrix over the entire image in various iterations to help in the calculation of the dot product of the original pixel values and weights.

Typically, this is followed by a layer of pooling which converts the size of an image into a low dimensional matrix.

How Deep Learning Enhances Machine Vision

Digitization has great grip on industrial production with processes automated as part of the industrial Internet of Things (IIOT). When it comes to IIoT also known as Industry 4.0, different machines and robots pick on the majority of everyday production tasks. Take for example in assembly, new, compact and mobile robots like collaborative robots work hand in hand with their human colleagues.

The IIoT's highly automated and universally networked production flow features a machine-to-machine interaction based on the machine vision to correctly identify a wide variety of objects in the flow of goods in factories and the entire chain process. Machine vision improves the efficiency and safety of the above workflows and has become an indispensable device for engineers who want to automate and speed production.

As of today, innovation machine learning and deep learning process have created strong recognition rates. Thanks to the developments in artificial intelligence, companies have the ability to benefit from a higher degree of automation, greater productivity and correct identification, and handling of a wide collection of objects using the whole value chain.

Since the "eye of production", machine vision software has turned to be an important element of technology, processing unstructured data like digital image and video produced by cameras to select objects by their external optical features alone. This particular software works fast and attains a high and reliable identification rate. Additionally, it is applied in a wide range of tasks like fault inspection and automatic handling of objects in robotics.

Analyze and Assess Large Data Sets

In an effort to make sure that the identification process is robust and adaptable to the requirements of networked IIoT processes, machine vision software developers increasingly depend on methods from the branch of artificial intelligence. Deep learning is a branch of machine learning that allows computers to get trained and learn via architectures such as convolutional neural networks (CNN).

The specific feature of AI, deep-learning, and machine-learning technologies is that it is analyzed in detail and evaluate large amounts of data to train a lot of classes and effectively distinguish between objects. Additionally, this particular data is produced within IIoT.

To apply deep learning, CNNs has to be trained. This particular training process associates to specific external features which are typical of the object such as texture, shape, color, and surface structure. The objects are classified into various classes depending on the above properties to assign them more precisely.

Train Objects Using Classification

How exactly does the training process work? The user will first supply image data which has been provided with labels already. Then, every label corresponds to a tag which defines the identity of the specific object. The system shall analyze this particular data, and based on this produce "trains" which are similar to the models of the objects recognized.

As a result of the following self-learned object models, the deep learning network can be able to assign the newly-added image data to the relevant classes like their data content. As such, the items can continue to be recognized automatically.

A simple image for direct comparison is no longer relevant for each individual object. After all, deep learning processes can learn from new things independently. By accepting features of all image data, conclusions can be extracted from properties of a given class, which considerably enhances the identification rates. This process is referred to as "inference."

And so, deep learning algorithms are very good for optical character recognition (OCR) applications that are accurately identifying number or letter combinations. Because of the extensive training process, the general feature of individual characters is exactly identified depending on the classes defined. But because there are a lot of different fonts, others with deviating features like serifs, problems can emerge assigning them with certainty.

Reduce Excessive Training Time

Companies avoid using AI-based technologies like deep learning because of their complexity. They need developers to have a great expertise. The training process usually calls for a lot of sample images to identify objects.

More than 100,000 comparison images might be required for every class to accomplish the right recognition rates. Although the relevant sample data is present, the training process usually picks a huge amount of time. Typically, the programming work for recognizing different defect classes at the time of fault inspection are often complex. The reason is that highly skilled employees with the right training are needed for this purpose.

The modern machine vision solutions that have a large number of deep learning functions can assist. The new version of the standard software MVTec HALCON allows companies to train convolutional neural networks without a great deal of money and time. At the end of the day, the software is installed with two networks which are optimally pre-trained for industrial use.

Therefore, the training process operates only with a few sample images supplied by the customer and they are customized to the customer's exact applications. This generates neural networks which can be accurately compared to the customer's individual requirements.

User companies can highly cut down the amount of programming work required by systematically categorizing new image data and saving time and money. Typically, they don't have any in-depth AI expertise. Companies can involve their current personnel without issues to train the network.

Identify Defects Efficiently

Recognize problems in a time-consuming process because the appearances of defects like tiny scratches on an electronic part can be accurately described in advance. As a result, it is hard to manually launch suitable algorithms which can recognize any conceivable faults depending on sample images. An expert may require to manually see hundreds of thousands of images and programs an algorithm which describes the error as accurately depending on this observation.

Deep learning technologies and CNNs, on the other hand, independently train certain characteristics of defects and accurately define similar problem classes. And so, only 500 sample images are required for each class depending on which technology trains, verify, and therefore, detect the different types of defects classes. The self-learning algorithms help to hugely reduce recognition errors, even though the error quotas for manual programming can be quite high.

Chapter 5: Natural Language Processing

What is it and What is it Used For?

Artificial Intelligence (AI) is transforming how everyone looks at the world.
AI "robots" are everywhere. Right from our phones to devices such as
Amazon's Alexa, the current world is surrounded by machine learning.

Netflix, Google, video games, and data companies including many others
apply AI to help handle large amounts of data. The end result includes
insights and analysis that might have been difficult.

There is no surprise when different kinds of businesses are adopting large
companies' success by applying AI and jumping on the board. However, not
all AI is designed equally in the business sector, even though some types of
artificial intelligence are useful than others.

This chapter will look at Natural Language Processing (NLP). This is another
type of artificial intelligence that concerns on analyzing the human language
to develop insights, create advertisements, assists your text, and more.

Well, Why NLP?

Natural Language Processing is a new technology which powers most types
of AI that you always see. NLP is currently being applied in many different
sectors and that should show you how important it is. You can think of it this
way, every day, human beings speak thousands of words that other human
beings interpret to perform different things. At the center, it is just simple
communication, but we are aware that words run much deeper. There's a
specific context by which human beings derive meaning from everything a
person says, whether they mean something with their body language or in the
way they describe something. Although NLP doesn't rely on voice inflection,
it does derive contextual patterns.

This is the point at which its value increases. Let's apply an example to illustrate how powerful NLP is when it is applied in the practical situation. If you are typing on an iPhone just like the way many of us do daily, you'll see suggestions of words depending on what you are typing and what you always type. And that is called natural language processing in action. It is this little thing that many of us take for granted, and have been ignoring for years, but that is the reason why NLP becomes very important. Now let's bring it to the business world.

Let's say that a company wants to choose how best it can advertise to their users. They can opt to apply Google to identify common search terms which users type when they look for their product.

NLP will support for quick compilation of data into terms which are related to their brand and those that might not expect. Taking advantage of the uncommon terms might provide the company with the ability to advertise in new ways.

Well, How Does NLP Work?

As said above, natural language processing is a type of artificial intelligence which analyzes the human language. It exists in many forms, but at the center, the technology assists machine to understand and communicate with human speech.

However, understanding NLP isn't that straightforward. It is an advanced type of AI that has of late become viable. This means that not only are we just learning about NLP but also it is hard to grasp. The following is a breakdown of NLP in layman's term. This means that it is the easiest way to understand the way natural language processing works.

The first thing in NLP is based on the application of the system. Voice-based systems such as Alexa and Google Assistant have to translate words into text. That is carried out using the Hidden Markov Models system (HMM).

The HMM has math models that allow it to decide whatever you say and translate it into usable NLP system. Break that down, the HMM listens to 10 to 20 milliseconds clips of speech and searches for phonemes to make a comparison with a pre-recorded speech.

The next thing is the actual understanding of the language and context. Every NLP system has a really different technique but on the whole, it is fairly similar. The systems attempt to break every word down into parts of speech.

This often takes place through a series of coded grammar rules which depend on algorithms which incorporate statistical machine learning to assist in determining the context of whatever you speak.

If you are dealing with speech-to-text NLP, the system will skip the first step and jump straight to analyzing words using algorithms and grammar rules. The end result is applied in different ways.

For example, an SEO application might use a coded text to extract keywords related to a specific product.

Semantic Analysis

If you are discussing NLP, it is essential to break down semantic analysis. It is closely associated with NLP and one may even argue that semantic analysis allows the development of the natural language processing. Semantic analysis refers to how NLP AI can logically interpret human sentences. When the HMM method break sentences down into their standard structure, semantic analysis will permit the process to add content.

For example, if an NLP program searched for the word "DUMMY", it must have the context to check whether the text refers to calling someone "dummy" or it just refers to something else such as car crash.

When the HMM method breaks down the text and NLP supports the formation of human-to-computer communication, then semantic analysis offers room for everything to make sense contextually. Without the presence of semantic analysts, then AI could not have reached the current level.

Problems

The two major problems experienced in the natural language processing include:

1. The level of vagueness in natural languages.

2. The complex nature of semantic information existing in simple sentences.

Normally, language processors have to handle a large number of words, most of which have other alternative application and large grammar which supports the development of different types of phrases. Tools which process language are very complex because of the different types of vagueness and measure of irregularity.

Activities Involved in Natural Language Processing

A simple structure of NLP deals with four major stages. In an actual system, these stages don't take place as different, sequential processes. In this case, both syntactic analysis and semantic analysis are dealt with the same principle.

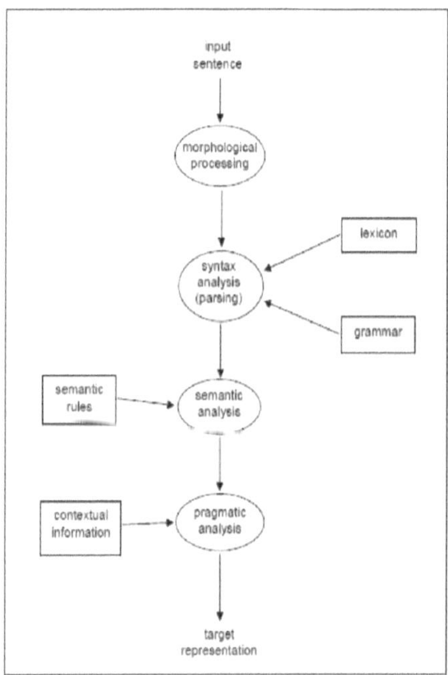

Morphological Processing

The focus of morphological processing is to divide strings of language input into a set of token that resembles discrete words, punctuation forms, and sub-words.

For example, a phrase like "unreal" is divided into two sub-word tokens such as un-real.

Morphology deals with selecting base words to create other words with the same meaning but different syntactic category. The modification takes place by adding a prefix and postfix but other textual changes can take place. Essentially, there are different word cases which lead to modification. That is inflection, derivation, and compounding.

A typical structure of morphological processing depends on the language being analyzed. This means that single words contain all information about the number of sentences, person, and tense. Other languages, this kind of information may spread across different words. For example, the English phrase "I will have been walking" contains a complex tense by just checking at the structure of the auxiliary verbs. Other languages link prefixes to nouns to indicate their roles while other words have inflections to display the proximity of information.

The English is very easy to apply morphological analysis and tokenize than other languages. These languages can have an ambiguous morphology that is resolved by performing semantic and syntactic analysis on the input. An example in English can be between plural and singular verbs.

The result from a morphological process consists of a phase of string tokens which you can apply for lexicon lookup. The tokens may contain gender, number, tense, and in some instances, it may have additional syntactic information for the parser. The next step of processing is called syntax analysis.

Syntax and Semantics

The device that deals with language processing has to perform several functions based on syntax and semantic analysis. The purpose of syntax analysis is to determine that a string of words is accurate and divide it into a structure which reveals the syntactic relation between words.

There is a tool called syntactic analyzer that performs the following with the help of a dictionary of word and a collection of syntax rules. A simplified lexicon might consist of syntactic classification of each word and a simple grammar. The example below includes a simple grammar and lexicon.

Lexicon

word	category
cat	Noun
chased	Verb
large	Adjective
rat	Noun
the	Article

Grammar

Sentence → NounPhrase, VerbPhrase[2]
VerbPhrase → Verb, NounPhrase
NounPhrase → Article, Noun
NounPhrase → Article, Adjective, Noun

Semantic and Pragmatics

The next stage includes pragmatics. Semantics and pragmatics are different. However, there is no universal difference between the two. Semantic analysis is mostly related to the meaning of words, while pragmatic analysis handles the outcome of a semantic analysis. For that reason, if you have a sentence like
"The large cat chased the rat" in semantic analysis can reveal an expression that means a cat but it can't explain more steps to help recognize the cat. That remaining part is left for pragmatic analysis. In other words, the task of pragmatic analysis is to disambiguate sentences that can't be fully disambiguated in the process of semantic and syntactic analysis.

How NLP is Changing Search and Customer Service

So far, you must have interacted with different virtual assistants such as Alexa and Siri. These have been designed to enhance customer service and automate specific tasks. Natural language processing is making artificial intelligence easy to communicate. In this section, you will learn these robots are redefining the customer service.

When Apple launched Siri for iPhone 4S in 2011, it was just a matter of time before other industries realized that speaking to our phones would change both the way we look for information online, plus how we interact with other devices.
However, most users were surprised in the way they used voice-recognition devices.

Voice-activated devices have become the new normal. In a study by the PWC, it indicated that consumers between the ages of 18 to 24 see themselves as "heavy-users" of NLP technology plus 57% of those above 50. And these users don't just chat with their devices but also use them to make purchase decisions. The NPD group discovered that purchasing an Echo, consumers could spend extra money on Amazon.

So what can companies do to ensure that they can be found by Siri? Let's look at the facts based on the Apricot Law's Tom Desmond. Traditionally, customers who used Google were presented with various pages and page results. However, voice assistants only presented one or two options.

But AI platforms attempt to respond to these queries in a human way, and they apply the text of pages in search results to do it. As a result, it is important for content to be optimized for a conversational language with a correct, clear grammatically answers to a particular question such as what, who, when, and why?

Building landing pages with a clear location have become very important than ever in the era of NLP and voice search.

Chatbots

Chatbots get a bad perception just because they are known as smooth female voices which prevent us from speaking to real human beings. However, many popular brands use Chatbots to elevate their customer service to the next level. For instance, Starbucks has applied AI to create a virtual barista. The My Barista app makes use of NLP technology to help users both order coffee through chatbot and predict what customers may want to order in future.

Google Duplex

Google introduced Duplex this year as a robot which has been designed to interact in a natural conversation.

Chapter 6: Recommendation System

We live in an era defined by the shift from traditional industries to an economy based on information technology. Thanks which are aware of the importance of the information they gather in a natural way.

This type of transformation doesn't take place without its own difficulties. For instance, each year the amount of information produced increases exponentially. About 90% of the data around the world has been created in the last two years.

This is about 2.5 quintillion bytes each day. That is 25 followed by 17 zeros every single day. While the world continues to be connected with the ever-increasing number of electronic devices, this amount of daily created data is set to increase in the coming years. If you are confronted with these massive amounts of information, any team of human analysts would be correctly overpowered. So what can organizations and companies do to take advantage of their valuable information?

One of the most recurring issues which have become very popular is how to decide the interest of customers in different contexts. When a company would want to sell a high volume of a specific product to a given audience, it has to dedicate its focus to the right group of customer. This is not simple, and that is noticed when you consider the number of users and products alongside the type of interactions that they might have. For instance, how is it possible to identify the type of items that are the best for a new user or how you can recommend products if there are no ratings?

Traditionally, just general and simple strategies were applied depending on factors such as gender, geographical location, and age. But these rules fail to include the value of the large information present about customers and products. It is not sensible to expect humans to scan through every single combination, something that may take decades. And so, the question stands, what should be done?

What is a Recommendation Engine?

Also known as recommender systems, its popularity started to rise in the retail industry, especially in online retail for customized product recommendations. One of the most popular applications is the Amazon's section on "Customer who bought this item also bought…" Recommender system refers to a smart and complex salesman who knows the taste and style of the customer. As such, it can make intelligent decisions focused on recommendations that would excite most the customer.

While it first started with e-commerce, it is now widely applied in many different areas. Examples include YouTube's "Recommended Videos" and Netflix's "Other Movies You May Enjoy." Other markets which have started to apply recommendation engines include the transportation industry. Here, IBM uses its control systems.

Essentially, what a recommendation engine does is to filter the data by applying different algorithms and predict the most important product to customers. The first thing is that it had to record the past actions of a customer and based on that recommend products which users might be interested to buy.

In case new users visit an e-commerce site, there will be no previous history of the user. In this case, the recommender system may opt to suggest the best-selling products to the customer. These are the kinds of products that most users buy when they come to the site. Another way is to recommend products which would produce the highest profit to the business. Being able to suggest different items to a customer based on their interests may develop a positive impact on the user. This has the benefit to make the customer make frequent visits to the same site.

As a result, many businesses are installing smart and intelligent recommendation engines by taking into consideration the behaviors of their users.

1. Data collection

The first step when it comes to building a recommender system is a data gathering process. The data can be gathered in two ways — implicit and explicit. Explicit data refers to that which is generated intentionally such as input from users and ratings of a movie. When data is implicit, it means the information is not presented deliberately but gathered from existing streams of data like order history, search history, and clicks.

2. Data Storage

The size of data will define the effectiveness of a recommendation model. For example, in a movie recommender system, the higher the ratings from a user, the better the recommendations become. This specific data is important in making a decision related to the type of storage applied. This specific storage consists of a standard SQL database and other types of storage objects.

3. Filtering data

Once you have collected and stored data, the next thing is to filter it so that you can get the correct information required to form the last suggestions. There are different types of an algorithm that you can use to make the filtering process easy. Below is a description of each algorithm.

Content-based filtering

Also known as cognitive filtering, it recommends items after comparing the user history and the content items. The content of every object is shown as a set of descriptors. The profile of the user is represented using similar terms and build by performing an analysis of items done by the user.

A few things have to be underlined while creating a content-based filtering system. The terms have to be automatically or manually located and a method selected to extract the terms from items.

Next, representing the terms such that is possible to compare the user profile and item correctly. Thirdly, the learning algorithm is chosen to learn and recommend items depending on the user profile.

How to choose a learning method?

The effectiveness of a learning method plays a critical role when it comes to choosing the method to apply. The most important thing is the nature of the complexity of the algorithm.

Storage requirements can be a major challenge since many user histories have to be maintained. Neural and genetic algorithms are usually slower than other learning methods. One reason is that iterations are needed to define whether a document is important. Instance-based methods reduce in effectiveness when a lot of training example is available. Some of the best to use include relevance feedback and Bayesian classifier.

The probability of a learning method to emulate the changes depending on the user's history is important. It is important for the method to assess the training data because instances last for a short time.

Collaborative filtering

It is also known as social filtering. In this approach, information is filtered using recommendations of other people. The major focus revolves around the concept that people who settled on the evaluation of specific items in the past are likely to come to an agreement in the future. An individual who wants to look at a movie, for instance, may ask for a recommendation from friends. The recommendations of some friends who share similar interests are more trusted compared to a recommendation from others. This type of information is applied to the type of movie to watch.

Neighborhood-based approach

Most collaborative filtering systems use the neighborhood-based approach. In this technique, different users are selected based on their similarity to the active user. A prediction for the active user is generated by computing a weighted average of the ratings of the chosen users.

To demonstrate how a collaborative filtering system can make a recommendation, consider the example of ratings in a movie table shown below. This table contains ratings of five movies by five people. A "+" shows that the person loved the movie and a "- "shows that the person did not like the movie.
To predict whether Ken would love the movie "Fargo", a comparison of Ken's ratings with others is done. In this situation, the ratings of Ken and Mike are similar and since Mike loved Fargo, one can predict that Ken would love the move too.

Movie ratings

	Amy	Jef	Mike	Chris	Ken
The Piano	–	–	+		+
Pulp Fiction	–	+	+	–	+
Clueless	+		–	+	–
Cliffhanger	–	–	+	–	+
Fargo	–	+	+	–	?

Rather than just waiting on the most similar person, a prediction is determined based on the weighted average of recommendations of different people. The weight assigned to a person is defined by the correlation between the people for whom to define a prediction. Just as a standard measure of correlation, you can apply the Pearson correlation coefficient.

Selecting neighborhoods

Most collaborative systems must be able to deal with a large number of users. Predicting something by using thousands of ratings by other people has grave effects on performance. As a result, if the number of users rises up to a certain number, then a selection of the best neighbors has to be performed. In this case, two techniques which can be used include the correlation-thresholding and best-n-neighbor. The first technique identifies only those neighbors whose correlation is higher than a given threshold.

Sparsity problem

While dealing with a lot of ratings can be a very big problem, systems that deal with few ratings trigger serious issues. This problem happens when the number of items is very large, thus reducing the number that users have rated to a small percentage. In this case, there is a chance that two people have few rated items in common which makes the correlation coefficient less reliable. This is called a sparsity problem. A wide variety of solutions have been designed to deal with this problem.

- **Implicit ratings.** There are systems such as later extension of GroupLens that attempt to increase the number of ratings by referencing them from the user's behavior. But still, a user has to identify an item before the system can deduce a rating.

- **Dimensionality reduction.** By cutting down the dimensionality of the information space, the ratings of two users can be applied in making predictions even if they didn't rate the same items.

- **Content description.** By selecting the content of an item instead of the actual item itself, this may increase the size of information that people share. This is a hybrid technique that is used to combine content-based filtering and collaborative filtering.

Item to item approach

This technique is an inversion of the neighborhood-based approach. Rather than measuring the similarities between people, the ratings are applied in measuring the correlation between items. The Pearson correlation coefficient can still be used as a measure. For instance, the ratings of the movies "Fargo" and "Pulp Fiction" have a perfect correlation.

Chapter 7: Internet of Things

All IoT devices need intelligent coordination and control. The last decade saw massive strides made in AI systems, to work together with IoT, no matter the differences.

AI appears to be the most interesting topic nowadays. There are a lot of talks and even misunderstanding and confusion about what AI is precisely and what is not. AI is affecting the current and future industries in the world. It is not running away and is likely to be more relevant as it grows.

The IoT describes ecosystem of discrete computing devices that use sensors connected through internet infrastructure. The idea could be rising up in the industry for some time, but the democratization of computing technology through affordability and availability of small computing devices pushed it to the mainstream.

With an increase in investment, a generation of new products, and the increasing tide of enterprise deployments, artificial intelligence is generating a wave in the Internet of Things (IoT).

Signals

1. The venture capital funding of AI is growing fast.

2. There is a high acquisition of AI focused IoT start-ups.

3. Big organizations across industries are already taking advantage of AI with IoT to supply new offerings and work efficiently.

The AI Key to Opening IoT Potential

Artificial intelligence contributes a big role in IoT applications and deployments. Both acquisitions and investments in startups which integrate AI and IoT have increased in the last two years. Key vendors of IoT platform software now provide combined AI capabilities like machine learning analytics.

The significance of AI in this particular context lies in its potential to rapidly wring insights from data. AI technology, Machine learning, provides the ability to automatically select patterns and identify anomalies in the data that intelligent sensors and devices supply information such as humidity, temperature, vibration, and sound. When compared to the traditional business intelligence devices that track numeric thresholds to be crossed, machine learning approaches can decide operational predictions up to 20 times earlier and with a great accuracy.
Other AI technologies include speech recognition and computer vision can assist in deriving insight from data. AI applications for IoT allow companies to escape unplanned downtime, spawn new products, increase efficiency, and improve risk management.

AI and IOT Working Together

Both AI and IoT have distinct histories but in the same evolution era. All of them started with an aim to boost legacy systems. For the Internet of Things, this refers to automating and improving available infrastructure and processes for better production and efficiency. When it comes to Artificial Intelligence, the original apps were built with a great emphasis on human-centered processes. Nowadays, the move is shifting towards an integrated IoT native and AI-native technique build from the ground ready for transformative digital methods. In most cases, new IoT solutions contain inbuilt features.

Some of the importance and improvements that AI brought include:

1. AI and IoT allow automation which disrupts the labor market by generating a demand for a new and different set of skills in many industries. Some of the industries transformed in the United States by the changing roles include accommodation, manufacturing, transportation, and food services.

2. AI and IoT are applied in the product to service-oriented business models. IoT provides business leaders with data that they may use to set up intelligent trade-offs. AI provides the intelligence needed to make the choices.

3. AI and IoT create new value propositions.

Role of AI and in the IoT

In the past year, artificial intelligence is a great necessity when you want to build and increase the number of sensor online devices. And it will even be more important when you want to create meaning from the data streamed from the same devices to help IoT revolution.

Quantified Self and IoT Revolution

The phrase "quantified self" makes us understand the start of the combination of IoT and Artificial Intelligence. In other words, quantified self refers to personal knowledge through self-tracking using technology. Are we living a good life? How can you improve it? Where should we save time?

You collect data in many different areas of life. You can analyze inputs such as the quality of air around us. You analyze different states of our mood. Sometimes we look worried about our mental and physical nature.

However, data is the most important resource for us because it can generate an action. This means that you need to collect and analyze data immediately to uphold a continuous flow of information. This is one of the major processes that result in the IoT revolution.

IoT Requires Artificial Intelligence

According to predictions of 2020, it is expected that there shall be many connected devices per person, data processed shall be in terabytes per second without counting in IoT. At a certain point, the internet of things shall be the largest source of data existing on the planet. And the IoT revolution can allow devices to highlight places that have opportunities.

Now, you can understand how information technologies support the transformation from old systems to advanced intelligent applications and services. To select the previous known pattern, it is important to generate a real-time data collection. But to find a method to work with this plus the data and information generated by these devices is a very big problem.

Artificial intelligence has attained a point where it can offer valuable help in speeding up tasks done by people. The moment computers can fully automate a human brain, it will result in an "intelligence explosion" that will radically change civilization. The speed of innovation shall increase exponentially. Artificial intelligence will definitely surpass the self-driving and aircraft.

AI as Part of IoT Revolution

IoT is currently creating a huge haystack of data. Many organizations are finding it difficult to make some meaning from the big amounts of data. About each large corporation is collecting and maintaining an extensive size of human-oriented data related to customers, including their purchases, preferences, and other personal information.

To conclude, the internet of things refers to data that flows between devices. To find these needles in the haystack, you must use artificial intelligence. In a few years to come, artificial intelligence can be an important element of any IoT system.

Conclusion

Artificial Intelligence and technology are one area of life that will continue to interest and surprise us with new topics, products, innovations, and new ideas. What was considered at a certain time as dumb machines have become smarter to the point where people can communicate with them on a human level. By combining with companies and other systems on their behalf, artificial intelligence makes everything that it touches smarter, and by learning as it moves on, it improves its own usability.

For companies and businesses to take advantage of AI-powered and improved interactions, the conversation has to begin inside the organization. Leaders are supposed to start with the available channels and improve their smartness. From that point, they are supposed to ask key questions about engagements with customers and employees.

The current interfaces depend on user interface design with a general limiting factor. It is significant to train the UI team to make use of AI technology and re-think interfaces without screen limitation. Much more than just another tool to assist in generating value, AI is not about how your company does things—it's who you are. In the end, we've learned AI definition, brief history, computer vision, and many more AI topics. This is not the end of AI, there is still more to learn from AI. Who knows what AI can perform to us in the future — maybe it will be a society of robots.

9 798456 392244